THE GEOMETRIC KINGDOM
RUPERT LOYDELL
&
MARIA STADNICKA

Newton-le-Willows

Published in the United Kingdom in 2020
by The Knives Forks And Spoons Press,
51 Pipit Avenue,
Newton-le-Willows,
Merseyside,
WA12 9RG.

ISBN 978-1-912211-76-0

Copyright © Rupert Loydell & Maria Stadnicka, 2020.

The right of Rupert Loydell & Maria Stadnicka to be identified as the author of this work has been asserted by them in accordance with the Copyrights, Designs and Patents Act of 1988. All rights reserved. No part of this publication may be reproduced, stored in a retrieval system, transmitted in any form or by any means, electronic, photocopying, recording or otherwise, without prior permission of the publisher.

Acknowledgements:

Some of these poems have been published by the following magazines and online journals: *Amethyst Review*, *I Am Not A Silent Poet*, *International Times*, *Osiris*, *Otata*, *The Poet's Republic*, *Prototype* and *Stride*.

Thank you Anne-Marie Cummins, Daisy Dimmock, Rachel Fitzpatrick, Alina Grindei, Helen Hawke, Stella Maile for our meaningful conversations. Thank you, Mark Mawer, for yet another opening. Thank you, Alec Newman, for your keen eyes and editorial guidance.

Thank you Horatiu Ioan Lascu, David Scott Milton, Rick Vick and Reuben Woolley for the beautiful words you sent me before you entered your geometric kingdom.

THE GEOMETRIC KINGDOM

Contents

The Ruin of Here	9
Shoreline	10
Because	11
Spring Cleaning	12
Headline	13
Distant Thunder	14
Dissenters' Burial Ground, Ponsharden	15
Cartagena	16
Invocation	17
Karenin	18
Traffic	19
Warrior	20
M5	21
Continuum	22
Rigor Mortis	23
Closing Night	24
Habitatum	25
Half-awake	26
State of Execution	27
Nothing to Give Us a Sense of Volume	28
Onion	29

Journal Page	30
True Colours	31
Thought	32
Moth Kingdom	33
Ensemble for Two Pianos	34
Now's the Time	35
Zoom	37
Beyond	38
Objects	39
Relay	40
Cher Papa	41
Silences	42
Eyelid	43
Live for Today	44
Punctus Contra Punctum	45
Genius	46
Final Dispositions	47
End of the Line	48
Minor Voice	49
Urban Afterlife	50

'I have wrestled with death. It is the most unexciting contest you can imagine. It takes place in an impalpable greyness, with nothing underfoot, with nothing around, without spectators, without clamour, without glory, without the great desire of victory, without the great fear of defeat, in a sickly atmosphere of tepid scepticism, without much belief in your own right, and still less in that of your adversary. I such is the form of ultimate wisdom, then life is a greater riddle than some of us think it to be.'
    – Joseph Conrad, *Heart of Darkness*

'What reconciles me to my own death more than anything else is the image of a place: a place where your bones and mine are buried, thrown, uncovered, together. They are strewn there pell-mell. One of your ribs leans against my skull. A metacarpal of my left hand lies inside your pelvis. (Against my broken ribs your breast like a flower.) The hundred bones of our feet are scattered like gravel. It is strange that this image of our proximity, concerning as it does mere phosphate of calcium, should bestow a sense of peace. Yet it does. With you I can imagine a place where to be phosphate of calcium is enough.'
    – John Berger, *And Our Faces, My Heart, Brief as Photos*

The Ruin of Here

'the future is a monotonous instrument'
 – Frances Picabia, 'Blind Man's Bluff'

But we still want to get there,
try to climb the stairs too early,
reach the lighted birds, escape
the ruined castles of our lives.

It looks as though they are flying
but it is only projected shadows
on the bare stone walls. It seems
there is a way out but there isn't:

these earth steps will crumble,
turn the power off and the light
will fade. We are not suited
to the dereliction of today.

Rupert Loydell & Maria Stadnicka
Shoreline

At the funeral of a woman I know
I see her earlobes have been
stripped of pearls. Her right temple
rests at an angle on picture books,

still, monochrome like in old snapshots.
The graveyard's blues swirl
with greens. Water meets land
in seashells between her fingers.

Gales crush against the creases
of her dress, clouds dangle
off the church ceiling. I ask if she
has ever learnt to build a boat.

No. Never. What would I need it for?
She smiles from a distance
at the child I am breastfeeding.

Because

Because they live longer lives
   we let them sleep all day
   then die alone.

Because they do not understand
   we cannot teach them,
   prefer not to talk.

Because they do not earn enough
   we let them eat badly
   and live somewhere else.

Because they are not us
   we are not interested
   and leave well alone.

Because they will die sooner
   we make excuses
   and put ourselves first.

Because we do not understand,
   they are always there;
   thankfully somewhere else.

Because we do not care
   they are not cared for,
   and live on their own.

Because they live such lives
   we push them away
   and let them die alone.

Rupert Loydell & Maria Stadnicka

Spring Cleaning

Tuesday with dust shining on jars,
sitting on cracked lino to watch Clara
piling old memories in black bags. Cleaning day.

Up and down the stairs, one-winged sister
trips over my legs but keeps singing.
The tune slides across walls, butterflies jump
from her mouth on her head then out.

I wonder what butterfly meat tastes like,
if sliced with a silver blade; what mother tasted like
the moment I was released – honey coated pearl.
I smell the skin on my wrists to see if mother is hiding in there.

'Remember the day she left to buy bread?' I tell Clara,
'She had stilettos, a hat, mid-eighties permed hair.'
Grown long to her ankles by now.

Clara sets fire to old carpets,
fibres curl, briefly spark, die off in smoke.
Baby dolls rest on rubbish bin's lid.
The house fills with mid-eighties permed ashes.

Headline

Late at night, the sidewinds pushed a car
off the road. They made an emergency stop.

No city in sight, nor visible lights. They could not
see a landmark in the rear-view mirror.
Just absence and floods.

Between treetops, one of them noticed
a planet hanging down, tilted off balance.
Went out to get a closer look of its shadow.

The further he went, the deeper the quicksand.
The earth sobbed, shooting star came to life,
he stepped out of view.

Rain washed away the return of her captive.

Rupert Loydell & Maria Stadnicka
Distant Thunder

Hard, cold and dead:
icy flash and flicker,

semi-darkness between.
Over the liquid surface,

the image of the present,
contours of forgotten things.

Doors are open to
the darker side of dawn,

hidden stories and presences,
stone and mud, fresh blood.

Dissenters' Burial Ground, Ponsharden

The cracked language of stones
all askew and fractured,

moss-edged, ivy-clung,
on the edge of land & town.

We try not to disturb kaddish,
tread carefully around the dead.

Rupert Loydell & Maria Stadnicka

Cartagena

When I collected my father's ashes
at the crematorium
I thought to keep them hidden
in a pencil case.

The undertaker handed back
his old beer-stained passport
and postcards from cities
he had planned to visit one day.

That night, in my hotel,
I fell asleep in his clothes, dreamt
a room filled with journeys and ink.

Father's hand moved across maps
and pointed the Danube, the Volga,
the sea with its blackness.
Smoky seeds ready for new soil.

I jumped awoken by rain on a wet deck.

Invocation

What is the function of invocation, what
do we hope to achieve? Grotesque rituals
as a form of ghost dance, dodgy seances
with incoherent messages from the dead,
do not constitute a resurrection machine.

When people listen to themselves what
do they hear? Years of silence, whispers
of brutality and inner selves. Help us
to reconfigure and confuse, to stay alive
and respond to the command interface

you specify. Death is a Möbius strip
of lies and decay, so what keeps you
going now you have abandoned life?
Emails from the living, kind eulogies,
and traces of self-evident decay.

In the beginning we invoke the one,
but now we are struggling to breathe.
What is the function of elucidation,
transformation, the idea of the divine?
Something to cling on to as we die.

Rupert Loydell & Maria Stadnicka

Karenin

not long after doctors decide to stop treatment,
I feel hair locks growing inside my lungs

/a footnote, not headline/

asphyxia, earthquake, someone younger
lost at sea pushes his way out through my vocal cords

poison, drowning, mute wedding photo watches
from the bedside table in my hospital room

at this point, John Coltrane appears on stage
to play 'Giant Steps' as a nurse breaks free

from the audience she asks me to sign
a disclosure agreement before turning off
life support.

/falling, the hydrogen bomb does not have
time to ask the victims of their age/

the day closes, enters the geometric kingdom:
ctrl alt delete

Traffic

It was the longest sun
and it swerved left-right left-right,
hit pedestrians watching a bullfight.

On the opposite lane,
a runner in standby, reading *Nausea*;
his baby wailed in a pram chewing a rifle.

It looked like the gun fired at me:

The bullet hit the edge of my book
then sank into earth like a poem
dropped from a bridge.

Urban rumours carried on
indicating an obstacle in the road.
Childless vehicles, late for work.

Nobody looked ahead,
nobody looked behind.
My shadow jumped on a live grenade.

The city emptied.

Rupert Loydell & Maria Stadnicka

Warrior

I watch the funeral pyre on TV burn
and imagine the stink of human flesh.
Bill always used to laugh with us about
wanting a Viking funeral on the creek –
a warrior on fire drifting out to sea,
or to leave his corpse out for the birds;
of course we took him to the crematorium,
same as everybody else. Does planning
our own departure help those left behind
or give us some vestige of control
from beyond the grave? We joke, too,
about haunting those we love, a threat
made in vain as we choose the poems
and songs we want used to say goodbye.
I've now lived longer than my father,
step into the unknown years he never did.

M5

After a power cut, waterlogged hours
unravel dimming dark threads.

The motorway's in stand still.

A wonder-bird drives past
the Suspension Bridge,
leaving the nest to defend itself.

Sleet gets through her dress,
gropes her heart's corner.

Roadworks keep the candlelight going
for sleepy men digging out earth;
mother-wings fly off
towards something uncertain.

Here, distance is all that matters,
before the absolute stop.

A stranger at the steering wheel, in free fall.

Rupert Loydell & Maria Stadnicka
Continuum

The bird has a key
plucked from
a headless stone angel.

Spirit ascends
to unlock the future.

Rigor Mortis

I am nobody. A blind pigeon jumps
click-clack click-clack on the roof
concerto for one instrument

it drops a letter for me, up
on the landing, a long-lost
Rembrandt cheers me up

its heartbeat stares into space

I have no followers and I follow no one.
I eat the supper in silence,
polish my armour click-clack.

My beak touches the ground.

Rupert Loydell & Maria Stadnicka

Closing Night

The last gasping breath
from a failed experiment,

a desert animal caught
swimming across the sky.

We always had something to say
but no one to say it to;

this unmarked grave
was not dug willingly.

They, them, us. Goodbye.

Habitatum

I live at the top floor,
in a flat with a view
to a perfect car park.

I take white little stones
and place them, like pills,
in straight lines on my desk.

Through a hole in the sky,
I watch the beheadings
going on in the city
and point a fully-loaded gun
against the world.

My earth rests, suspended
between wild heavens
and landscaped gardens.

The sun hangs loose
above silent bell ropes
as if nothing has happened.

Rupert Loydell & Maria Stadnicka

Half-awake

In morning dreams I made a collage
of all the people I have known who died
(think Peter Blake and *Sgt. Pepper's* ...),
lined them up with my previous cats
squatting at the front. It was easy
to start with, but I didn't know where
to stop. How many acquaintances,
friends of friends, and people
I hardly knew, should I include?
The crowd stretched out of view.

In the centre, aunts and uncles,
my father and grandparents,
were reunited. My parent's friends
that I'd known as a child, friends'
parents, and that aunt who wasn't
really an aunt, along with famous
pop stars and writers I'd mourned.
What to do with the cut-out dead?
Start forgetting and they'd disappear,
blow hard they might fall down.

Who'd really changed my life, who
had I cried for when they died?
The picture changed immediately,
group shrunk to a manageable size.
The usual suspects: a few I'd always
loved, some I realised late how much
they'd meant to me, friends killed
in accidents. Lost dreams became
fading maps of my relationships
with those no longer here.

State of Execution

It simply dawns on me.
The minute I'd touched
her memory
a fortress collapsed.

'the blood is gushing for shelter'

Death does not talk.
It pulls my trousers up,
it hides me under a stone.

Rupert Loydell & Maria Stadnicka

Nothing to Give Us a Sense of Volume

He watched her fade in the distance,
versifying the end of her life:
a kind of happiness that was inexplicable.

Things you don't understand: runaway music
constructed from samples and loops, phones
going off every five minutes to say nothing.

Sinking into the waters of sadness
complicates the flow of faster currents;
the time for navigation has run out.

Experts in subliminal communication
affirm the direction of your death.
The stars didn't look back.

Every summer she recalled her childhood,
brief sanctuary, the blessing of an ending.
He was never any good at tying knots.

Onion

The world as places and sounds, a visual music to paint. Hidden layers are stories to be told, ur-texts and brief asides, all referencing each other. It is not a linear progression, our futures do not unfold; we make them, revise them, retell them, practice making others laugh. Then move away and die.

Gaps in the curtain, wing and a prayer, everybody knows

Rupert Loydell & Maria Stadnicka

Journal Page

We inhabit the world's pipeline
picking up fallen apples, friends who
died of battlefield injuries turned into
slowly burned paragraphs,

churches modelling new prisons,
floating prayers from cell to cell
damp kiss proof that we are enemies.

Beneath the viewpoint air currents force
tired birds into submission,
from our enclosure we like watching
the fall talking about ourselves

pretending to see the whole in
small incisions below the continuum.
In truth, knowing too much about
the ferocious nature of man.

True Colours

Abstract works, fire at night:
probably not a direct reference.

Dark places no brighter than
flickering flames on the horizon;

the hours round midnight
associated with death.

Dress well and be yourself:
emotionally distant,

disinterested and sterile,
with a streak of deals and debts.

Soundtracks to other lives
make a nonsense of this world.

Maybe there's no such thing
as the way it will turn out to be,

only grace and expectation,
dirty moon and autumn light.

Rupert Loydell & Maria Stadnicka
Thought

When the truth eventually came out
they said all the vital preparations were made.

Something essential stopped her half-way.
Late, almost there, almost present.

If she had waited a bit longer,
someone would have noticed
the sudden passing of such a short miracle.

Moth Kingdom

In the Moth Kingdom everything
is blurred and dusty, undefined.
Mistakes are honoured and upheld,
background becomes foreground
and every idea takes gentle flight.
It is always twilight, never dark
or light enough and everything's
aflutter. Things have grown too tall,
too large, looking for the light.

Rupert Loydell & Maria Stadnicka
Ensemble for Two Pianos
(to Clara and Luca)

At first, I counted heartbeats, my ears watched
for sudden changes in atmospheric pressure
and planetary alignments. Night cries squeezed
the cords of my flesh until milk-tears would burst.
Primal hunger kept us awake. I got used to
saving the last mouthful for somebody else.
In crowds, I walked ahead, my elbows made space
for a wider view and a wider earth.
Time watched us.
When bedtime arrived, I touched twin backs
with my fingertips, covered you both, promised
'I'll keep you safe.' Those words I said
before candles turned off. Time already knew
you would leave by morning.

The Geometric Kingdom

Now's the Time

This is yesterday's news today, or possibly
tomorrow's news from yesterday. You
have brought the Sunday papers round,
oblivious to the fact we read online
and that this feels like *déjà vu*. I wonder
if Ingmar Bergman was right? Will I be
'a better ghost than I am a human being'?
I'll let you know. In the meantime
there's the tennis or football to watch,
and politics to ignore. Democracy
is dying but that is nothing compared
to Richard, Dad or my other friends
who are not with us any more. This
is old news too, but it makes me cry
when I think about the people gone.
There are rows of cracked stones in
the cemetery near home, but I have
nowhere to grieve, because we burn
the bodies now. Lucy said some people
carry on emailing the dead, holding
a one-sided conversation; others say
they commune and speak with their
loved ones. I think it's a bit of a joke,
but then I've spent years grieving
for people I hardly knew but wished
I had, and for those I knew well
who have gone. You can try and live
for the now but there's a sense of
repetition, a relentless concern with
getting ahead, of keeping up and
using each day before it disappears.
It will, I know, however much time
is just a constructed idea we use
to bully and persuade ourselves
there are more things to do.

Rupert Loydell & Maria Stadnicka

The world won't end without us,
it's us who will disappear, whatever
we do to try and make our mark.
For me it's words and paintings,
others run fast or eat the most pies.
We're all going to be forgot.

Zoom

In the back of a car,
a thought held his hand,
adjusted his glasses

did I die in a crash?
or maybe they waved
from a bedroom window;

the words multiplied,
the ropes played with children
but none of us had

the courage to move closer
for fear of making too much noise.

He had recently taken up chess.
When the bullet hit, he was
planning the next move

between two windowpanes,
a shortcut to heaven. The
mid-giggle blast, rotating

stuck in familiar music box
stood out flour trace leading us
to a crime scene.

Out of the cinema,
the crowd felt slaughter
and rushed to unsee, unhear.

The blinds were drawn.
The camera zoomed in.
The lullaby malfunctioned.

Rupert Loydell & Maria Stadnicka

Beyond

Hostile polarization and extensive paramilitarism,
ideological confrontations and bloody terrorist attacks.
She uses that tension and channels it into her work:

rich textures, dream sequences and subterranean music,
a catalogue of rejected clichés and jokey asides,
recreate the world that never was, could never be.

But here we are today, each with a label on our back,
so that others can know our name. Beyond death's door,
evening is growing dim and gossip cannot hurt us now.

Objects

Tomorrow lived in the same house with us;
bursts of yellow-red heated mute water pipes,

afternoons passed lettering names,
we'd exchange poems for shoes we bought
at the market.

There were no written instructions for happy
until a bailiff came to collect your dresses and scarves.

I gently obliged and made tea.

Tomorrow has now departed in high heels,
vanished behind the walls of right-here-right-now.

Rupert Loydell & Maria Stadnicka

Relay

Here in the present, we document the past
and imagine what will happen next.

Fascinated by spaceships and planes, the possibility
of drought and destruction, we feel we're missing out.

Death gets in the way of us all;
we can only run and hand the baton on.

Cher Papa

I did not know how much
you wrapped yourself around my heart
until today when sitting in the park
I accidentally caught you eating bread.

You took each bite with eyes closed,
gently stroked the crust
like you would do, on Sunday, at church.

You did not smile; it was the sun
who smiled back, for a brief moment.

I had been there, in the cold, for quite a while,
and did not move or blink or even breathe.
Just waited.

You packed the crumbs away
and vanished. And then I sobbed.

Rupert Loydell & Maria Stadnicka

Silences

When I came to write this, I had lost the first sheet of paper written in the night as the poem nudged at me, escaping from the book I'd finally managed to read after three attempts.

The story is told to the narrator by his friend ('I remember he said that she said'), slowly recounted by the author. It is a book about the recent past, history and how people escaped it, ran away or hid, allowed others a place on the train or a plane. It continues until we get to facts about extermination, concentration camps, memory and loss.

Between the words, the silence, says Dan Beachy-Quick, each silence as nuanced and potent as the rest. Untold stories need telling, but we need room for the unsaid too, space to write and think.

Death happens all too soon.

Eyelid

Everyone said I was looking in the opposite direction
when the car hit.
The sun was high, beginning of the longest day.
Crowds covered the scene with blankets,
dropped coins on my eyelid.

The traffic stopped and a sandwich maker
made the sign of the cross in the air,
came closer to watch.

For some time, unreturned call echoed in dust.

A week later, news got to you.
A body was found by the railway station.

Rupert Loydell & Maria Stadnicka

Live for Today

I am trying to read about death
and our attitudes to it; to listen
to the radio discussing a musician
whose name I haven't heard yet.
It's impossible to juggle and balance
any more: life is too complicated
and I enjoy too much. Music, books,
art and film – I want to see and listen
to them all. The music on my radio
repeats and changes, changes
and repeats, chimes into Sunday.

It's Monday and the pianist plays on.
I don't want to move, don't want to
live here, need to go right away;
any day is as good as any other day
for dreaming and planning my escape.
Life's too short and we trap ourselves
with money, houses, things. I have
little to my name, am caught in
revision and reworking of the same.
Today is shot to pieces and time
is running backwards, standing still.

Punctus Contra Punctum

From time to time,
we stand between
a wolf and a dog. We germinate
inside tightly zipped handbags
falling into a moment of muteness.

We are expected to root
given the choice of death.

A step closer, a level higher
in a battery operated game:

nobody comes in
without prior agreement.

The recoiled bows springs out
unleashed by a howl.

At a steady pace
we catch a moving train.

Rupert Loydell & Maria Stadnicka
Genius

He built a resurrection machine
to bring back all the dead.

We can hardly move in the village
for corpses and lost relatives

crowded in the streets. They don't
understand today or where they are,

can't eat or drink, will die again
and then again. Time stinks.

Final Dispositions

Perhaps if I suddenly died
for just a feather

it could be, I suppose, due to
an algorithmic error.

Sad, I know, at this age
not to realise that

such a weight would
actually cost my life and

probably regret a bit
the misunderstanding.

But only a bit.

Rupert Loydell & Maria Stadnicka

End of the Line

Is this what dying is like? Creeping around
in the quiet early morning, before the sun
cuts through the low cloud and burns
the dew off the abandoned garden chairs
and yesterday's overheated debris? We can
hope it's that simple and painless, easy
to transfer without any passport queues
or scans for unwanted items; or be real
and know it will be something or nothing
else. But let's hope heaven is as scruffy
as our overgrown lawn here, and not
our neighbours' suburban fuss; that
the ferry trip brings us to wilderness
and new lands, though one hopes there'll
be a coffee shop and somewhere to sit
and sup. It's likely that heaven has now
given in to commerce and we will have
to pay the dead to simply become dead,
get used to smartening up if we want
to be considered for the choir. Perhaps
death is more like tripping down the steps,
hands full, scream lodged in our throat;
or simply drowning in the summer air
as it becomes too hot and starts to
undulate and move. Or life might simply
stop.

Minor Voice
(to Robin Wheeler)

I saw a man leaving a water glass
at a junction where the elm tree,
he used to know,
had been suddenly cut down.

He showed me it did not hurt
when something you love
gets replaced by a shadow.

An overnight rain came
out of nowhere, swallowed
the wood, the roads
and everything vanished.

Rupert Loydell & Maria Stadnicka

Urban Afterlife

After a funeral, paperwork sits
in boxes at the end of desk rows.

Undertakers pause to change
suits before shift handover,

diesel engines flatten down
places of rest. Glass, iron, gravel.

Machines know: cities grow
in negative spaces, oil traces gift

buildings with signs of the cross.
Gliding hawks operate traffic

for clear passage. Night drops
its guard; machines argue,

power cuts add imagination
to people's lives. So much

for ending day's work seeking dawn.

Rupert Loydell & Maria Stadnicka
About the Authors

Rupert Loydell is Senior Lecturer in the School of Writing and Journalism at Falmouth University, the editor of *Stride* magazine, and a contributing editor to *International Times*. He is a widely published poet whose most recent poetry books are *Dear Mary* (Shearsman, 2017) and *A Confusion of Marys* (Shearsman, 2020). He has edited anthologies for Salt, Shearsman and KFS, written for academic journals such as *Punk & Post-Punk* (which he is on the editorial board of), and contributed co-written chapters to books on Brian Eno and *Twin Peaks*.

Maria Stadnicka is Associate Lecturer in Sociology at University of the West of England, Bristol and PhD researcher in psycho-sociology, exploring intergenerational socio-cultural trauma transmission. She is a contributor to *International Times* (UK), *Dissident Voice* (US) and her work is published in literary journals and magazines in Australia, Austria, Canada, Mexico, Morocco, Romania, UK and US. She is the author of *Imperfect* (2017), *The Unmoving* (2018), *Bearings II* (2019), *Somnia* (2020) and the forthcoming collection *Buried Gods, Metal Prophets* (2021).

www.ingramcontent.com/pod-product-compliance
Lightning Source LLC
Chambersburg PA
CBHW022125040426
42450CB00006B/858